Poetry and Painting

Baudelaire, Mallarmé, Apollinaire, and their Painter Friends

ALAN BOWNESS

The Zaharoff Lecture for 1991–2

CLARENDON PRESS · OXFORD

This book has been printed digitally and produced in a standard specification in order to ensure its continuing availability

OXFORD
UNIVERSITY PRESS

Great Clarendon Street, Oxford OX2 6DP

Oxford University Press is a department of the University of Oxford.
It furthers the University's objective of excellence in research, scholarship,
and education by publishing worldwide in

Oxford New York

Auckland Cape Town Dar es Salaam Hong Kong Karachi
Kuala Lumpur Madrid Melbourne Mexico City Nairobi
New Delhi Shanghai Taipei Toronto
With offices in
Argentina Austria Brazil Chile Czech Republic France Greece
Guatemala Hungary Italy Japan South Korea Poland Portugal
Singapore Switzerland Thailand Turkey Ukraine Vietnam

Oxford is a registered trade mark of Oxford University Press
in the UK and in certain other countries

Published in the United States
by Oxford University Press Inc., New York

Reprinted 2011

ISBN 978-0-19-815198-2

Printed and bound in Great Britain by CPI Antony Rowe,
Chippenham and Eastbourne

POETRY AND PAINTING: BAUDELAIRE, MALLARMÉ, APOLLINAIRE, AND THEIR PAINTER FRIENDS

It is a striking fact that the three men who successively did so much to create modern French poetry—Baudelaire, Mallarmé, and Apollinaire—were all deeply responsive to the visual art of their contemporaries, and had many painter friends. There is no precedent for this in any earlier phase of French literature, nor do we find anything that is comparable in the parallel literary cultures of Germany or England. In England, it is true, one notices another strange particularity, not found elsewhere, that of the painter-poet, equally at home in two arts. Blake and Rossetti are the obvious examples, and Wyndham Lewis and David Jones in the twentieth century. Victor Hugo is the nearest the French come to this, but his paintings scarcely challenge his writings. What is much more characteristic across the Channel is the way in which French contemporary painting and visual culture generally exist as a real presence for all the writers of the period from the 1840s onwards. My three poets are the most obvious, but others—Gautier, Zola, Huysmans, Proust, Valéry—are further testimony to this French response.

Baudelaire was from childhood enthusiastic about painting; 'ma grande, mon unique, ma primitive passion',[1] as he wrote in his journal. 'Goût permanent, depuis l'enfance, de toutes les représentations plastiques.'[2] Soon after he came of age, in the autumn of 1843, Baudelaire moved into his own rooms in the Hôtel Lauzan on the Île St Louis. This was to be the first and only apartment which he could decorate as he wished. The place of honour was given to a copy of Delacroix's *Femmes d'Alger*.[3] The original hung in the Palais du Luxembourg where work by living French artists was on public exhibition, and the copy was made, no doubt at Baudelaire's request, by the young painter, Émile Deroy.[4]

[1] He speaks of 'le culte des images', not specifically of painting, see C. Baudelaire, *Mon cœur mis à nu (Journaux intimes)*, in *Œuvres complètes*, ed. Claude Pichois (Paris 1975–6), 2 vols., i: 701.

[2] Ibid.

[3] F. W. J. Hemmings, *Baudelaire the Damned* (London 1982), 48.

[4] It is not however listed among the copies of the *Femmes d'Alger* cited in Lee Johnson, *The Paintings of Eugène Delacroix* (Oxford 1986), iii. 165–6.

Deroy was Baudelaire's first artist friend. They were exact contemporaries, both born in 1821, and, as far as we can see, very close in the years 1843–6 when Baudelaire wrote his first art criticism, the *Salons* of 1845 and 1846. Also hanging in Baudelaire's Hôtel Lauzan apartment was the portrait which Deroy painted of his friend. This was submitted to the 1846 Salon, but was refused. Shortly afterwards Deroy died, aged 25.[5]

Deroy inevitably remains a shadowy figure, but I suspect that Baudelaire owed him a great debt. Any writer on art who is not a practitioner himself needs such a guide.

Another friend in the Hôtel Lauzan circle tells us that at this time Baudelaire was as much preoccupied with painting as with poetry.[6] The *Salon* of 1845 was of course his first published work, and when his inheritance was withdrawn to be replaced by a modest and inadequate monthly allowance Baudelaire perhaps saw writing on art as a way of earning a living. The problem was that his own tastes in painting were, and remained, limited, and conventional, in the sense that the artists about whom he wrote so brilliantly were already established figures. His enthusiasm for Haussoullier's *La Fontaine de Jouvence* at the 1845 Salon is exceptional, and sits very strangely with that sudden, final demand for someone to paint the heroism of modern life, to celebrate the coming of the new. Baudelaire never again championed in print a contemporary or younger painter, although, as we shall see, the two outstanding artists of the next twenty years were his close friends.

Art critics often write best about painters half a generation older than themselves, and this is certainly true of Baudelaire and Delacroix. Delacroix, born in 1798, was twenty-three years older than Baudelaire, who saw himself as Delacroix's champion, placing him in the poem, *Les Phares*, in the sequence of the greatest masters of art.

We do not know exactly how and when they met, nor how close their friendship really was. The introduction probably came soon after Baudelaire's *Salon* of 1845 appeared in print. No artist can resist fervent young admirers, but one suspects Delacroix kept his distance. There are few references to Baudelaire in his *Journal*, which unfortunately does not exist between 1832 and 1847.

The first (and most interesting) entry is on 5 February 1849. Delacroix records that Baudelaire called and talked of the difficulties

[5] The painting is now in the Musée de Versailles. [6] Ernest Prarond.

Daumier was having finishing his oil paintings, and then 'il a sauté à Proudhon qu'il admire et qu'il dit l'idole du peuple. Ses vues me paraissent des plus modernes et tout à fait dans le progrès'.[7]

It is interesting to note that when Baudelaire called Delacroix was at work making a half-size version of the *Femmes d'Alger*.[8] The original, which Baudelaire had praised so warmly in his *Salon* of 1846, is an altogether singular work in Delacroix's œuvre, in that it is not a historical, biblical, allegorical, literary, or political statement, but simply documentary realism, allied to pure painting. This point was made at the picture's first showing in 1834 by Gustave Planche, an excellent writer on art, who said: 'c'est de la peinture et rien de plus, de la peinture franche, vigoureuse . . . une hardiesse toute vénitienne'.[9] The *Femmes d'Alger* does of course represent a line of descent from Giorgione's *Concert champêtre* in the Louvre, which Delacroix loved and had copied.

Just as Delacroix had turned away from violence after the *Mort de Sardanapale*, so after the *Femmes d'Alger* he never again made such a bold statement of modernity in an exotic setting. Until his death in August 1863, at the very moment of the Salon des Refusés, he preferred to concentrate his energies on large-scale decorative schemes for public and semi-public places, a kind of withdrawal from the action which might have demanded too much of him. Baudelaire in his 1846 *Salon* had called Delacroix the head of the *modern* school, and one can argue that it is with the *Femmes d'Alger* that modern art begins. It has remained a talismanic picture, copied by Renoir and Picasso, very much alive to us today though its colours have sadly darkened.

Baudelaire wrote far more about Delacroix than he did of any other painter, and there are perhaps two reasons for this obsession, one personal and one poetic.

Baudelaire's father, François, died in 1827 at the age of 68 when his son was 5 years old. He was passionate about the fine arts, could draw and paint, commissioned statues and paintings for the Luxembourg Palace where he was employed as steward, collected himself, and filled his apartment with 27 sculptures and over 200 paintings, mainly by his first wife. This was the environment in

[7] E. Delacroix, *Journal*, ed. A. Joubin (Paris 1950), i. 258.

[8] Now in the Musée Fabre, Montpellier, a gift from Courbet's friend, Alfred Bruyas, who won it in a lottery in 1851.

[9] Quoted by Lee Johnson, *The Paintings*, 169.

which Baudelaire grew up as a small child, and it all disappeared with his father's death. It is hard not to see Baudelaire's adulation of Delacroix in part as the creation of a father substitute. 'Le génie n'est que *l'enfance retrouvée* à volonté', wrote Baudelaire in *Le Peintre de la vie moderne.*[10]

Delacroix was also the immediate poetic precursor whom Baudelaire could not find in contemporary French literature. A schoolfriend tells us that at twenty Baudelaire was passionate about old sonnets (Villon and Ronsard) and the newest painting.[11] This reminds us of the conversation between Housman and Gide at Cambridge in 1917, when Housman suggested that there was no tradition of French poetry, and that between Villon and Baudelaire there was rhymed discourse in French literature but no poetry.[12]

It was poetry that Baudelaire found in Delacroix, especially in such works as the *Femmes d'Alger.* In his writing on art, Baudelaire kept returning to Delacroix, and in the final obituary essay in 1863 he emphasizes his role as a *literary* figure, a great reader, more mourned by poets than painters, and above all 'le traducteur émouvant de Shakespeare, de Dante, de Byron et d'Arioste'.[13] In other words the crucial figure in the international literary tradition to which Baudelaire felt he belonged.

What is the special, mysterious quality about Delacroix's art, Baudelaire asks. 'C'est l'invisible, c'est l'impalpable, c'est le rêve, c'est les nerfs, c'est *l'âme,* et il a fait cela—observez le bien, monsieur—sans autres moyens que le contour et la couleur . . . Delacroix est le plus *suggestif* de tous les peintres.'[14]

As so often, when Baudelaire writes of Delacroix one feels that he could be writing of himself. And when Delacroix in his *Journal* talks of art as a fragile veil drawn over the terrible emptiness of the soul of man one has the first statement of an attitude to which both Baudelaire and Mallarmé would have subscribed.[15] The programme for the symbolist painters, Gauguin and Redon, is here being adumbrated.

It is time to move on to Baudelaire's other painter friends. Deroy died in 1846, and in 1847 Baudelaire met Gustave Courbet, his

[10] C. Baudelaire, *Curiosités esthétiques,* ed. H. Lemaire (Paris 1962), 462.

[11] Charles Cousin, quoted in F. W. J. Hemmings, *Baudelaire,* 33.

[12] Mentioned by Wallace Fowlie in his excellent introduction to the Bantam Books bilingual edition of *Les Fleurs du mal* (New York, 1964), 1.

[13] *Curiosités esthétiques,* 426. [14] Ibid. 424.

[15] I quote from Lee Johnson, *The Paintings,* vol. iii, p. xiv.

senior by less than two years. I have written elsewhere about the relationship between Courbet and Baudelaire, and can only summarize here.[16] They were closest in the years 1848 to 1851—the turbulent years of the February revolution, the Second Republic and the establishment of the Second Empire. It was at this time, probably in 1849, that Courbet painted the famous portrait of Baudelaire which shows the poet taking refuge in the painter's studio.[17]

In the *Salons* of 1845 and 1846 Baudelaire had thrown down a challenge to the young painter: to paint the heroism of modern life. But how was this to be done? I believe that in 1847–8 Courbet tried, on at least three occasions, to paint a modern allegory that would meet Baudelaire's prescription. An echo of this abortive style can be seen in Courbet's 1848 cover design for the second number of the four-page radical magazine, *Le Salut public*, of which Baudelaire was co-editor. Note too Courbet's debt to Delacroix.

Courbet did go on immediately to create a new modern style, which we now call realism. When he returned to Paris in the summer of 1850 he brought back with him an enormous canvas, *L'Enterrement à Ornans*, which he showed at the Salon of 1850. Baudelaire had written in the 1846 *Salon* of the beauty of modern dress, even at its most sombre, because, as he said 'nous célébrons tous quelque enterrement'. Courbet had gone away and painted that funeral, a family affair on a heroic scale, but Baudelaire was silent about the result.

By the time Courbet came to paint the even larger *L'Atelier du peintre* in the winter of 1854–5, Baudelaire and Courbet had drifted apart, largely because Courbet was spending more and more time away from Paris. In his subtitle Courbet asserts that the painting is an 'Allégorie réelle déterminant une Phase de Sept Années de ma Vie artistique', and Baudelaire had to be given his place among Courbet's friends and supporters on the right side of the painting. Courbet originally included Baudelaire's mulatto mistress, Jeanne Duval, in the painting, but then painted her out, perhaps at the poet's request. Her shadowy profile is now dimly visible again.

Baudelaire's rather equivocal brief comments on Courbet in his pamphlet on the 1855 Exposition Universelle suggest that he had no

[16] A. Bowness, 'Courbet and Baudelaire' in *Gazette des Beaux-Arts* (Paris, Dec. 1977), 189–99.

[17] The painting is now in the Musée de Montpellier. A date earlier than 1849 or very late 1848 is unlikely in my opinion.

imaginative understanding of the new kind of art that Courbet was producing, but by then Baudelaire had come to regard all contemporary art as decadent and second-rate. In any case he was no doubt preoccupied preparing *Les Fleurs du mal* for publication. A group of eighteen poems had appeared under this title in 1855, and then the book itself with a hundred poems in 1857. It brought Baudelaire notoriety and fame, confirmed when the second, enlarged edition was published in 1861. By this time Baudelaire's creative career was nearing its end, and he wrote nothing of consequence after 1863. His health had begun the slow decline that was to lead to paralysis and eventually death in August 1867, at the age of 46.

We know that Baudelaire was briefly in Honfleur to see his mother in July 1865. Courbet spent the summer and autumn on the Normandy coast at nearby Trouville. I sometimes wonder if Courbet heard about Baudelaire's sad state. It is interesting that when Courbet returned to Paris for the winter he painted the most Baudelairean of all his pictures *Le Sommeil*, done for a private client, and also known as *Les Dormeuses*, *Les Amies*, and *Paresse et luxure.* The red-haired model was Joanna Hiffernan, the mistress of Whistler—'mon élève', as Courbet called him—who had also been at Trouville in the summer of 1865.

Baudelaire had written appreciatively of the young Whistler's Thames etchings in 1862, in his short essay, 'Peintres et Aquafortistes', mainly in support of Manet and Legros. And we know from a letter that Fantin-Latour wrote to Whistler that Baudelaire found *The White Girl* 'charming, exquisite, absolutely delicate' when it was shown at the Salon des Refusés in 1863.[18] There was no close friendship between the two men, though they do both appear in Fantin-Latour's *Hommage à Delacroix* of 1864, the first of Fantin's five group portraits. Delacroix had died on 13 August 1863, and the young painter, then aged 27, conceived the idea of a group portrait of his admirers. He did not at first think of including Baudelaire among the painters and critics, but no doubt Manet insisted. It is to Manet that we must now turn, for he carried forward the poet's ideas on modernity and the new, translating them back into the visual media.

Baudelaire and Manet met in 1858. They soon became close friends, and the intimacy lasted until April 1864 when Baudelaire left

[18] From an unpublished letter in the Library of Congress, quoted in Gordon Fleming, *The Young Whistler* (London 1978), 189.

for Brussels. Manet's first important picture, *Le Buveur d'absinthe*, rejected at the 1859 Salon, is very Baudelairean in feeling, and may be an illustration to a poem in *Les Fleurs du mal.* Almost every painting by Manet from now until 1864 can be related to Baudelaire's ideas. The poet was writing his essay on the illustrator, Constantin Guys, between 15 November 1859 and 4 February 1860, though it was three years before he could find a publisher. (He wrote an article on Daumier in 1861, but again could not get it published, and the article is lost.)

Though entitled *Le peintre de la vie moderne*, the essay is not about painting. It is an affectionate portrait of an artist nearly twenty years older than Baudelaire. There is a real perverseness in the fact that when, after fifteen years, Baudelaire comes to name the painter of modern life he should choose a *petit maître* of modest ambitions. A remarkable contrast exists between the tone of Baudelaire's essay and the great poem that he also wrote in 1859, 'Le Voyage'. Baudelaire knows that he is nearing the end of his own life:

> Ô Mort, vieux capitaine, il est temps! levons l'ancre.
> Le pays nous ennuie, ô Mort! Appareillons!
>
> . . .
>
> Nous voulons . . .
> Plonger au fond du gouffre, Enfer ou Ciel, qu'importe?
> Au fond de l'Inconnu pour trouver du *nouveau*!

It was Baudelaire's friendship that gave Manet the encouragement to plunge into the unknown to find the new, and in doing so to become the true painter of modern life. *La Musique aux Tuileries* is a new kind of painting; the subject (and the composition) is a Guys drawing,[19] as interpreted by Baudelaire in his essay: the artist's 'passion et sa profession, c'est d'*épouser la foule*. Pour le parfait *flâneur*, pour l'observateur passioné, c'est une immense jouissance que d'élire domicile dans le nombre, dans l'ondoyant, dans le mouvement, dans le fugitif et l'infini'.

This is what Manet paints, as if instructed by his friend who accompanied Manet daily to the Tuileries Gardens while the paint-

[19] Perhaps *Aux Champs Elysées*, now in the Musée du Petit Palais, Paris, and formerly owned by Baudelaire. It is illustrated in Lois Boe Hyslop (ed.), *Baudelaire as a Love Poet and other Essays* (Philadelphia and London 1969), which also contains an important and often neglected essay by L. B. Hyslop and F. E. Hyslop, 'Baudelaire and Manet: A Re-appraisal', to which I am indebted. The quotation that follows is from Baudelaire, *Curiosités esthétiques*, 463.

ing was in progress. He appears at the extreme left, fashionably dressed, talking to Gautier. In the final paragraph of his 1845 *Salon* Baudelaire had stated that the true painter for whom we are waiting would be the one who could find an epic quality in contemporary life and make us understand 'combien nous sommes grands et poétiques dans nos cravates et nos bottes vernies'. This is exactly what Manet has achieved.

Manet was already described publicly in 1863, not as 'élève de Couture', his teacher, as was customary, but as 'élève de Goya et de Charles Baudelaire'.[20] Baudelaire had always been passionate about Spanish painting, and when the Spanish dancers arrived in Paris in 1862 he encouraged Manet to introduce a Spanish flavour into his own art. Among the results was a large painting of gypsies, which Manet destroyed. He made an etching of the subject which Baudelaire praised in his last published art criticism, the article on 'Peintres et Aqua-fortistes' of 1862, already mentioned, saying that 'le génie espagnol s'ést réfugié en France'.

For another of Manet's Spanish paintings, the portrait of the dancer, Lola de Valence, Baudelaire put into practice another early suggestion. In the 1846 *Salon* he had said: 'Le meilleur compte-rendu d'un tableau pourra être un sonnet ou une élégie'. Unfortunately Baudelaire's quatrain, provided for the etched version of the painting, is uninspired *vers de circonstance.*

The supreme examples of Manet's Baudelairean painting are of course the *Déjeuner sur l'herbe*, shown at the Salon des Refusés in 1863, and *Olympia*, shown at the 1865 Salon. They outraged public and critics, but in so doing established Manet as the outstanding painter of his generation.

The *Déjeuner* is, deliberately, a further transposition of Giorgione's *Concert champêtre*, with Delacroix's Algerians replaced by contemporary Parisians. *Olympia* too stands firmly in the tradition of great painting, notably the reclining female nudes of Titian and Goya. Manet is again responding directly to Baudelaire, who in *Le peintre de la vie moderne*, suggests that to paint a courtesan of today inspired by a courtesan by Titian is to invite only something 'fausse, ambigue et obscure'. Manet proves that this need not be the case, by painting a quintessentially Baudelairean woman, as for example in *Les Bijoux*:

[20] Description by the critic Monselet, quoted in Enid Starkie, *Baudelaire* (London 1957), 422.

> La très-chère était nue, et connaissant mon cœur,
> Elle n'avait gardé que ses bijoux sonores.

Everything about *Olympia*—the negress, the cat, the jewels, the shocking nudity—stand witness to the friendship of poet and painter. These are two of the greatest paintings of the nineteenth century. Manet was in his early thirties when he painted them, and never did anything so spectacular again.

I have spent much of my time talking about Baudelaire because he established what I see as a close and necessary connection between French art and literature. We now have the beginnings of a clear line of descent that passes from Delacroix to Baudelaire and then to Manet, and this is the genesis of modernism. Let us now more briefly follow it through.

The first defence of the new painting was undertaken by Émile Zola in newspaper articles, and then in *Edouard Manet: Étude biographique et critique*, published in 1867. Zola was eight years younger than Manet, and an intimate of Cézanne's, whose voice and opinions can be heard behind all of Zola's writings on art. Though Manet painted a superlative portrait of the young novelist the two men never became close friends. That position was reserved for another writer of the same generation, the poet Stéphane Mallarmé, born 18 March 1842, and thus exactly ten years younger than Manet.

They met in the latter part of 1873. Mallarmé was an obscure teacher of English in a Paris *lycée*, still little known as a poet; Manet a notorious painter. Temperamentally they were much alike: detached, reticent, sceptical. They were near neighbours in the new *quartier* behind the Gare St Lazare, and it became Mallarmé's daily practice to call at Manet's studio on his way home after teaching. In 1885, two years after Manet's death, Mallarmé wrote to Verlaine: 'J'ai, dix ans, vu tous les jours mon cher Manet, dont l'absence aujourd'hui me parait invraisemblable.'[21]

At the beginning of their friendship Mallarmé wrote two articles in defence of Manet's painting: this is his first writing on art. 'Le Jury de peinture pour 1874 et M. Manet' concentrates on the three pictures that Manet showed at the 1874 Salon. Much longer and more wide-ranging is 'The Impressionists and Edouard Manet', published

[21] S. Mallarmé, *Correspondance*, ed. Henri Mondor and L. J. Austin, ii (Paris 1965), 303.

in English in the *Art Monthly Review* of September 1876. It made little impact.[22]

The collaboration continued in two illustrated books: in 1875 an edition of Poe's *Raven*, translated by Mallarmé with six lithographs by Manet, which may be seen as a joint tribute to Baudelaire who had done so much to make Poe known in France. This was followed by the first publication in an *édition de luxe* in 1876 of *L'Après-midi d'un faune*, written, like so many of Mallarmé's few poems, some ten years earlier. Manet provided four tiny illustrations. The portrait of Mallarmé by Manet was painted in this same year.

Through his friendship with Manet, Mallarmé came to know all the leading impressionist painters: Renoir, Degas, Monet, and especially Manet's sister-in-law, Berthe Morisot, for whose posthumous exhibition in 1896 Mallarmé wrote a preface. The ten years of their intimacy were not, however, a creative period for Mallarmé. Then after Manet's death in 1883 the publications suddenly begin to appear, until with the *Poésies* in 1887 Mallarmé's position as the outstanding poet of his generation is assured, and symbolism triumphs over impressionism.

After Manet's death, Whistler became Mallarmé's closest painter friend. They met properly in 1887, when Whistler was again spending more time in Paris, and finding the artistic climate a good deal more sympathetic to his art than it had been in the 1860s or 1870s. Monet introduced them, and Mallarmé was attracted at once by Whistler's dandified appearance and his subtle and suggestive art. 'Je n'ai créé mon œuvre que par *élimination*' Mallarmé said in a letter of 1867, and this is equally true of Whistler.[23] Whistler persuaded Mallarmé to translate his artistic credo, the *Ten O'Clock Lecture*, and there followed an increasingly intimate friendship until Mallarmé's death in 1898. Whistler drew and painted the family; he provided the frontispiece for *Vers et Prose* in 1894. The strange nymphs that he painted at the end of his career found a place in Mallarmé's affections.

Whistler was among the regular attenders at Mallarmé's *mardi*

[22] I wrote briefly about this article in a short essay, 'Manet and Mallarmé', published in the *Bulletin of the Philadelphia Museum of Art* (April–June 1967), 213–19. Mallarmé's writings on art are reprinted in Penny Florence's excellent study: *Mallarmé, Manet and Redon* (Cambridge 1986).

[23] S. Mallarmé, *Correspondance*, ed. Henri Mondor, i (Paris 1959), 245. Rosemary Lloyd draws attention to this phrase in the valuable introduction to her *Selected Letters of Stéphane Mallarmé* (Chicago and London 1988), p. xix.

salons. He had a special place, as in Fantin-Latour's painting. At the end of Mallarmé's life, in the famous *salle à manger*, hung a group of paintings which expressed the poet's artistic sympathies: two Manets, a Morisot seascape, a Whistler nymph, a Redon pastel of flowers, and a Gauguin woodcut of the profile head of a Tahitian.[24]

The two younger artists, Odilon Redon, born 1840, and Paul Gauguin, born 1848, represent the movement away from impressionism towards a new art that we uneasily label symbolism. This came to the fore around 1890, as far as the visual arts were concerned. Gauguin was the *chef d'école*, seeking to overturn established values. Atheistic, confronting the death of God, he too deserves Sartre's description of Mallarmé: the poet of nothingness.[25]

Gauguin never became a close friend, but he was an artist whom Mallarmé admired greatly, without perhaps feeling the personal sympathy he had for Manet and Whistler. A mutual friend, the young poet Charles Morice, asked Mallarmé in 1891 to persuade the leading art journalist Octave Mirbeau to write an article on Gauguin. Mallarmé did so, in his letter praising Gauguin: 'Cet artiste rare, à qui, je crois, peu de tortures sont épargneés à Paris, éprouve le besoin de se concentrer dans l'isolement et presque la sauvagerie. Il va partir pour Taïti, y construire sa hutte, et y vivre parmi ce qu'il a laissé de lui là-bas, y retravailler à neuf, se sentir'.[26] Mirbeau agreed; the article appeared, and it was used again for the catalogue of the sale of his work that Gauguin held to raise money for his expedition to Tahiti. In gratitude he etched a portrait of Mallarmé.

Mallarmé was unfortunately ill, and did not go to see Gauguin's exhibition, but he presided at the farewell banquet for Gauguin, and was the first to speak, proposing a toast: 'Messieurs, pour aller au puis pressé, buvons au retour de Paul Gauguin; mais non sans admirer cette conscience superbe qui, en l'éclat de son talent, l'exile, pour se retremper, vers les lointains et vers soi-même'.[27] One senses a certain admiration for Gauguin's courage in renouncing a civilized existence, something Mallarmé could never have done.

On his brief return from Tahiti in 1893–5 Gauguin called on Mallarmé to tell him something of his voyage. He showed his

[24] Henri Mondor, *Vie de Mallarmé* (Paris 1941), 643.

[25] I quote the English title of Jean-Paul Sartre, *Mallarmé or the Poet of Nothingness* (Philadelphia and London 1988), translated and introduced by Ernest Sturm, though the original French text appeared as *Mallarmé: La Lucidité et sa face d'ombre* (Paris 1986).

[26] Mallarmé, *Correspondance*, iv (Paris 1973), 176–7; also in Lloyd, *Selected Letters*, 173.

[27] Mondor, *Vie*, 604.

Tahitian paintings in Paris, and Mallarmé was most impressed: 'Il est extraordinaire qu'on puisse mettre tant de mystère dans tant d'éclat.'[28]

In 1895 Gauguin left France to go back to the South Seas, never to return. The paintings that he made in the next two years are his most ambitious: we know now that they represent not a picture-book view of Tahiti, but an imaginative reconstruction of something that no longer existed. One cannot do without Eden, said Mallarmé in 1888; confronted with a void, Gauguin created a second Eden in his art.[29] His largest painting, *D'où venons-nous? Que sommes-nous? Où allons-nous?* was intended as a final statement before Gauguin took his own life. When asked in 1884 to define poetry, Mallarmé said: 'La Poésie est l'expression, par le langage humain ramené à son rhythme essentiel, du sens mystérieux des aspects de l'existence: elle doue ainsi d'authenticité notre séjour et constitue la seule tâche spirituelle.'[30]

The 'sens mystérieux des aspects de l'existence' is exactly what Gauguin is painting in *D'où venons-nous?* He sent the painting back to France, and it was shown in Vollard's gallery in 1898. There is an extraordinary letter which Gauguin wrote from Tahiti in March 1899 in which he seems to speak of Mallarmé's reaction. I quote from a probably corrupt text:

> Dans le large panneau que Gauguin expose, rien ne nous révèlerait le sens de l'allégorie, si . . . mon rêve ne se laisse pas saisir, ne comporte aucune allégorie; poème musical, il se passe de libretto (citation Mallarmé). Par conséquent immatériel et supérieur, l'essentiel dans une œuvre consiste précisément dans 'ce qui n'est pas exprimé: il en résulte implicitement des lignes, sans couleurs ou paroles, il n'en est pas matériellement constitué'. Entendu aussi de Malarmé devant mes tableaux de Tahiti: il est extraordinaire qu'on puisse mettre tant de mystère dans tant d'éclat.[31]

In Gauguin's absence in Tahiti, Mallarmé turned to the other leading symbolist painter, Odilon Redon. They had met early in 1885, through Huysmans. Sensing the poet's interest in his very idiosyncratic work, Redon sent him a copy of his *Hommage à Goya*, a portfolio of six lithographs.[32] Mallarmé wrote to thank him:

[28] Gauguin's letter to Mallarmé is printed in the *Lettres de Gauguin*, ed. M. Malingue (Paris 1946), 250. Mallarmé's comment is quoted by Gauguin in a letter to André Fontainas of March 1899, ibid. 288.

[29] Mallarmé's remark is quoted by Rosemary Lloyd, *Selected Letters*, p. xvii.

[30] Mallarmé, *Correspondance*, ii (Paris 1965), 266.

[31] *Lettres de Gauguin*, 288.

[32] Often reproduced, including in P. Florence, *Mallarmé*, plates 53–8. Florence is very good on the Mallarmé—Redon relationship.

Comme vous me gâtez! et venez au devant d'un de mes souhaits, qui était de regarder longuement une œuvre de vous. Voilà deux jours que je feuillette cette suite extraordinaire de six lithographies, sans épuiser l'impression d'aucune, tant va loin votre sincérité dans la vision, non moins que votre puissance à l'évoquer chez autrui.

Mallarmé goes on to give Redon his response to each plate: 'La tête de Rêve, cette fleur de marécage, illumine d'une clarté qu'elle connaît seule et qui ne sera pas dite, tout le tragique falot de l'existence ordinaire'.[33]

Mallarmé and Redon were united by similar temperaments and a desire to take their art into the unknown, to express the inexpressible. The two men spent summers together, and Geneviève Mallarmé was godmother to Redon's son. When Redon passed through a religious crisis and lost his faith in 1895 Mallarmé must have been a sympathetic friend. In his last summer at Valvins Mallarmé was planning a de luxe edition of his latest poem, *Un coup de dés jamais n'abolira le hasard*, and Redon was preparing the lithographs that were to illustrate it.

Mallarmé's death intervened, and the book never appeared. But the posthumous edition shows clearly how Mallarmé's concern with the visual presentation of poetry had taken a leap forward, from the more-or-less conventional text of *L'Après-midi* to the typographical simultaneity of *Un coup de dés*. Mallarmé dreamed of a future in which 'the world is made to end in a book', and his notes towards this end—the creation of the ultimate masterpiece—were published to a largely uncomprehending audience in 1957. This was a part of Mallarmé's deconstruction of language, and it led him into the abstract.

My third poet, Guillaume Apollinaire, had no direct contact with Mallarmé or his painter friends, though Mallarmé was an early influence on his own poetry. Born in 1880, he seems always to have been interested in painting, and he published his first article on art when in Germany in 1902.[34]

What is particularly striking about Apollinaire is not so much the actual content of his writings on art (which were to be considerable) as his extraordinary feel for new talent. Almost every innovatory

[33] Mallarmé, *Correspondance*, ii (Paris 1965) 279–80.
[34] Guillaume Apollinaire, *Chroniques d'art*, ed. L.-C. Breunig (Paris 1960), 20–1.

painter from 1904 until 1918, the year of his death, was known personally to Apollinaire who championed the work in print.

The process began, characteristically, with a personal contact. In 1904, Apollinaire, walking along the banks of the Seine near his mother's house in suburban Le Vesinet saw André Derain painting. Through Derain he met Vlaminck, and then Dufy and Braque—the group that, with the older Matisse, were to become notorious as the 'fauves' at the Salon d'automne of 1905.

It was the painters of this group who provided the illustrations for Apollinaire's first publications: Derain for the strange poetic reverie, *L'Enchanteur pourrissant* in 1909, and Raoul Dufy for his first book of poems, *Le Bestiare*, in 1911. Following Mallarmé's example Apollinaire liked to present his poetry in exquisite, illustrated editions. *L'Enchanteur* was published by Kahnweiler, the young German-born art dealer who represented Picasso—it was also his first *livre d'artiste*. Picasso should have illustrated *Le Bestiare*, and seems to have begun work on the project. Why it was passed on to Dufy we may never know.[35]

Apollinaire had met Picasso in October 1904, and this friendship was to be one of the most important in the history of art. In his excellent biography of Picasso, John Richardson devotes a chapter to what he calls the Apollinaire period (not the rose or pink period) which is from 1904 to 1906; he correctly says that Apollinaire 'exerted an immeasurable influence on Picasso's imagination and intellect'.[36] Both men were looking for a way out of symbolism, into a more classic and abstract art. Apollinaire almost certainly suggested a new subject matter to Picasso—the harlequins and *saltimbanques* of Picasso's pink period. Picasso's famous drypoint of Salome (1905) portrays Apollinaire as King Herod, and reflects exactly the lines that Apollinaire gives to Salome in his poem of the same name:

> Ne pleure pas ô joli fou du roi
> Prends cette tête au lieu de ta marotte et danse

Apollinaire shared the taste of all this generation of avant-garde artists for African sculpture, and collected it himself, as we know from the poem 'Zone'. He was not, however, able to follow Picasso as he worked on his grand statement of the new art in the years 1906

[35] Picasso—Apollinaire, *Correspondance*, ed. P. Caizergues and H. Seckel (Paris 1992), 80, n. 2.

[36] John Richardson, *A Life of Picasso*, i (London 1991), 334.

and 1907. The huge painting *Les Demoiselles d'Avignon* remained in Picasso's studio for special visitors to see, but Apollinaire is curiously silent about it.

Picasso in May 1907 introduced Apollinaire to a 22-year-old art student, Marie Laurencin.[37] They soon became inseparable, and the liaison lasted until June 1912 when she broke it off. In 1908 she painted a group portrait of herself with Apollinaire, and of Picasso with Fernande Olivier, and in the following year the untaught painter, Henri 'Le Douanier' Rousseau, painted her with Apollinaire as *Le Poète et son muse.* In his last years—he died in 1910—Rousseau suddenly found himself taken up by Apollinaire and his circle of painter friends, who admired the simplicity of his art.

Apollinaire knew Braque before the painter met Picasso in March/April 1907: he may have taken Braque to Picasso's studio to look at *Les Demoiselles d'Avignon.*[38] He praised Braque's *Grand Nu* as 'l'effort le plus nouveau' of the 1908 Salon des Indépendants, and went on to write the catalogue introduction for Braque's first important exhibition in November 1908 when proto-cubist pictures such as the *Arbres à L'Estaque* were shown for the first time.[39] Braque and Picasso were now working together, and went on to develop the language of cubism, moving closer and closer to abstraction. Braque's *Le Mandore* still life of 1910 suggests a direct reference to Mallarmé, and a visual equivalent of such poems as *Sainte* and *Une dentelle s'abolit.* The whole atmosphere of early cubism is Mallarméan in the way that early Manet is Baudelairean and rose-period Picasso Apollinairean. In cubism the work of art subsumes the subject, leaving the way open for abstraction. Braque remained devoted to Mallarmé, keeping a copy of the *Poésies* with him during his war service: Picasso, as a foreigner and an outsider, preferred Rimbaud.

Apollinaire recognized the extraordinary opening-up of painting which took place around 1910. He had found new friends in other painters of his own generation—Léger and Juan Gris, Robert and Sonia Delaunay, Gleizes and Metzinger, Picabia and Duchamp. These are the artists Apollinaire celebrates in his book of art criticism, *Les Peintres cubistes*, which appeared early in 1913. It is not a satisfactory text, too hastily cobbled together from earlier articles and

[37] Picasso–Apollinaire, *Correspondance*, 50, n. 20.

[38] Ibid. 80, n. 9.

[39] The articles are reproduced in G. Apollinaire, *Chroniques d'art*, 51 (a reference to the *Grand Nu*, though the footnote on p. 450 reminds us that we cannot be certain that the identification is correct) and 58–61.

fresh material. It should have been entitled *Méditations esthétiques*, as Apollinaire wished. A few weeks later, Apollinaire's collected poems appeared under the title *Alcools*, with a cubist Picasso drawing on the cover: the preparatory study for the painting of 1912, known as *Le Poète*.

Apollinaire was now a celebrated figure in the art world, seen as the champion of the new. He had close relations with the Italian futurists, introducing them to Paris in June 1913 with the third futurist manifesto, *L'Antitradition futuriste: Manifeste synthèse*, which proclaims 'mer . . . de . . . aux critiques, pédagogues, professeurs, musées . . .' and 'Rose aux Marinetti, Picasso, Boccioni, Apollinaire' and a long list of others, including Delaunay, Matisse, Braque, Derain . . . and R. Fry. As Apollinaire's fame spread, so his portraits multiplied, as an increasingly wide circle of artists wished to portray him, for example Chagall's *Hommage à Apollinaire* of 1912, and Giorgio de Chirico's premonitory portrait of 1914.[40]

Of Apollinaire's new enthusiasms, the most important for his own work was his friendship with Robert Delaunay and his Russian-born painter-wife, Sonia. When they met, Robert Delaunay was painting the enormous *Ville de Paris* (1910–12) and other works featuring the Tour Eiffel. His ideas of simultaneity, and his introduction of discontinuous modern imagery certainly influenced Apollinaire to compose 'Zone', the one strikingly modern poem that he placed at the beginning of *Alcools*:

> A la fin tu es las de ce monde ancien
> Bergère ô tour Eiffel le troupeau des ponts bêle ce matin

Apollinaire must have watched with increasing excitement as Delaunay brought primary colours back into his paintings, notably in the series of *Fenêtres* which occupied him in 1912. Apollinaire was inspired to pursue similar interests in a poem actually written in the painter's studio, looking out into the light, which he also called *Les Fenêtres* and saw as representing a totally new aesthetic:

> Du rouge au vert tout le jaune se meurt
> Quand chantent les aras dans les forêts natales

concluding:

[40] The catalogue of the exhibition, *Apollinaire ses livres, ses amis*, at the Bibliothèque historique de la Ville de Paris (June–Oct. 1991) gives further particulars of portraits of Apollinaire.

La fenêtre s'ouvre comme une orange
Le beau fruit de la lumière.[41]

Delaunay went on to paint light, in the series of *Disques* of 1912, which have a good claim to be the first abstract paintings. Apollinaire invented the word orphism to describe this new art of pure colour, and he writes in *Les Peintres cubistes*:

> On s'achemine ainsi vers un art entièrement nouveau, qui sera à la peinture, telle qu'on l'avait envisagé jusqui'ici, ce que la musique est à la littérature.
>
> Ce sera de la peinture pure, de même que la musique est de la littérature pure.[42]

If Apollinaire here seems to be championing an entirely abstract art, other friends of his, namely Picabia and Duchamp, were promoting an alternative modernism that would lead to Dada and surrealism. In *Les Peintres cubistes* Apollinaire speaks with admiration of Duchamp's paintings of 1912, such as the *Nu descendant un escalier*. He watched as Duchamp took cubist collage into new fields, such as the ready-made object presented as art, and the assisted and corrected ready-made, for example the advertisement for Sapolin enamel paint transformed into *Apolinère enameled* of 1916–17. Apollinaire shared Duchamp's iconoclastic spirit, describing his burlesque play, *Les Mamelles de Tirésias* of 1918 as 'une drame surréaliste', thus inventing the name that was to describe the leading avant-garde art movement of the inter-war years.

Apollinaire's own poetry had been affected by these further developments in painting. This is particularly noticeable in his concern for the visual appearance of his verse. First, in 1913, all the punctuation disappeared in *Alcools*, and then, perhaps following Mallarmé's typographic experiments in the *Coup de dés*, re-published in 1914, Apollinaire invented the calligramme. The collection that bears this title was published in 1918, with a portrait frontispiece of Apollinaire by Picasso. Not all the poems in *Calligrammes* are typographically innovative, and those that are range from the complex—the 'Lettre-Océan' that Apollinaire wrote to his brother in Mexico—to the charmingly simple falling lines of letters in 'Il pleut'.

Alas, not long afterwards, on 9 November 1918, Apollinaire died, a victim of the Spanish influenza epidemic. The adventure was over.

[41] See Francis Steegmuller, *Apollinaire* (New York 1963; the reference in the Penguin edn. (London 1986) is to p. 204.)

[42] G. Apollinaire, *Les Peintres cubistes* (Geneva 1950), 14.

In this lecture I have tried to construct a chain of friendships that binds together the art and literature, the painting and poetry, of what is certainly a great age of achievement in France. I have spoken about the three poets who were most deeply affected by the visual arts. It is an interesting progression, from Baudelaire, passionate about painting but not about the art of his contemporaries, to Apollinaire, who cared only for the new, with Mallarmé as the crucial central figure, who allowed the visual to change his work directly.

Much more could be said about their involvement, and of others attracted to painting—Valéry's admiration for Degas, one of the originals of Monsieur Teste; Proust's debt to Whistler, who may or may not be the Elstir of his great novel. The story continues—with Reverdy's long and close friendship with Braque; with the whole surrealist phenomenon, an interlocking of poetry and painting; with Michel Leiris's ongoing involvement with Picasso, Giacometti, and Francis Bacon.

Many questions arise. Is there a necessary connection between the arts? The concept of the *Zeitgeist* may not be easy to sustain, but evidence of personal interest in another art is a different matter altogether. Was the closeness of painting and poetry in this period a particular incitement to greater achievement? In my interlinked story you have been hearing about what might be called the genesis of modernism, but does this mean that the arts run parallel in any historical period? Something similar was surely happening in music, from Wagner to Debussy and then to Boulez. But then what happens if the arts move in a direction—towards increasing abstraction for example—which is to be more fruitful in painting than in poetry?

I do not intend to answer these questions, if indeed they are answerable. I am sure of one thing, however, and this is that no-one with a serious interest in the literature of this period can afford to neglect the visual arts, and no-one interested in the visual arts can neglect the literature.

The manufacturer's authorised representative in the EU for product
safety is Oxford University Press España S.A. of El Parque Empresarial
San Fernando de Henares, Avenida de Castilla, 2 - 28830 Madrid
(www.oup.es/en or product.safety@oup.com). OUP España S.A. also acts
as importer into Spain of products made by the manufacturer.
Printed and bound by CPI Group (UK) Ltd, Croydon, CR0 4YY

06/07/2026

02157628-0001